HAPPINESS is
HOMEMADE in
Door County

HAPPINESS is HOMEMADE in *Door County*

Recipes and stories by Karen Buhk

Photography by Sandy Buhk

HenschelHAUS Publishing
Milwaukee, Wisconsin

Published by HenschelHAUS Publishing, Inc.
www.henschelHAUSbooks.com
Milwaukee, Wisconsin

ISBN: 978159598-586-6
E-ISBN: 978159598-587-3
Library of Congress Control Number: 2018937485

Dedication

*Cooking is a gift to the given,
without expecting anything in return
except a smile.*

This cookbook was conceived one Christmas when my grandson Ryan said, "You should make a cookbook, Grandma. There are recipes and then there are Grandma's recipes."

With the help of his wife, Sandy, who took all the beautiful photographs, "Happiness is Homemade in Door County" has become a reality.

I got my nickname "Cookie Grandma" from my great-grandson Nathan. I got my passion for cooking from my mother, Alice, and my grandmother Christiana, whom we all called Jenny. My cooking skills were honed out of necessity; raising three hungry boys will make a cook out of anyone.

Thank you, Jim, Wayne, and John, for keeping me on my toes, for always having an appetite, and for all your love and support.

This book is also dedicated to my grandmother, Jenny Nissen Begotka
(May 1883–November 1961)

I loved my Grandma Jenny, my dad's mother. Her parents were from Denmark; her mother was of nobility and her father was the gardener's son. They fell in love and moved to America, where they made a life for themselves as farmers in rural Wisconsin.

Grandma Jenny and Grandpa John lived across the road from us. As a young girl, I followed Grandma Jenny all over, from driving her jeep out in the farm fields to helping her make all those delicious goodies. She was a free spirit and I loved spending time with her.

My mother, Alice, carried on her baking and taught me Grandma's recipes. Now you may enjoy her treats as well.

Recipes

Cakes

Apple Cake

I remember the smell of apple cake baking in the kitchen with my mother. It seems like yesterday. We had apple trees, so she made this in apple season, not like today when you can get apples all year 'round in stores. We were lucky to have a stay-at-home mother. She never worked outside the home, but had plenty to do with cooking, canning, and washing clothes with no dryer and hanging them outside all year long so they froze in winter. Life was hard, simple, and good.

CAKE
1 cup flour
2 teaspoons baking soda
½ teaspoon cinnamon
½ teaspoon nutmeg
A pinch of salt
1 egg, beaten
1 cup sugar
½ cup melted butter
2 cups diced apples
½ cup walnuts, chopped

CARAMEL SAUCE
½ cup brown sugar
½ cup white sugar
½ cup butter
½ cup cream

Preheat oven to 350 degrees. Grease an 8x8-inch pan with butter or cooking spray. In a large bowl, mix together flour, baking soda, spices, and salt. In a separate bowl beat egg, sugar, and melted butter until smooth, and then add the flour mixture. Fold in apples and walnuts. Pour batter into prepared pan and bake for 45 minutes. Let cool in pan.

Meanwhile, make caramel sauce. In a medium saucepan combine sugars, butter, and cream. Bring just to a boil. Cut cake to serve and drizzle with sauce.

Karen's Apple Cake

This is a great dessert for fall. One of my all-time favorites, best served with a scoop of ice cream or dollop of whipped cream.

CAKE
2¼ cups flour
2 teaspoons baking soda
½ teaspoon nutmeg
½ teaspoon cinnamon
¼ teaspoon cloves
A pinch of salt
1 cup white sugar
½ cup brown sugar
½ cup Crisco®
2 eggs
1 cup buttermilk
2 cups Macintosh apples,
    peeled and chopped

TOPPING
½ cup chopped pecans
¼ cup white sugar
¼ cup brown sugar
¼ teaspoon cinnamon

Preheat oven to 350 degrees. Grease a 9x13-inch pan. In medium bowl, combine flour, baking soda, salt and spices. In a medium bowl, cream white sugar and Crisco® until light and fluffy. Add brown sugar and mix until combined. Add one egg at a time and beat until well mixed. Add flour mixture alternating with buttermilk, scraping sides down as needed. Fold in apples. Pour into prepared pan.

Prepare topping, In a small bowl combine pecans, sugars, and cinnamon. Sprinkle over batter. Bake for 35 to 45 minutes, or until toothpick inserted at center of cake comes out clean.

Banana Cupcakes
with Peanut Butter Frosting

This is one of my go-to recipes that was handed down from my grandmother Jenny and my mother Alice, who made it for me on my birthday every year. It has become a big favorite of some of my grandkids, especially Rachel, Ryan, and David. I once made 36 of these for Rachel's class in school—that was a very big job.

CAKE
2½ cups flour
1 teaspoon baking powder
1 teaspoon baking soda
A pinch of salt
¾ cup Crisco®
1½ cup sugar
2 eggs
3 overripe bananas, mashed
1 teaspoon vanilla
1 cup buttermilk

FROSTING
3 cups powdered sugar
½ cup unsalted butter, softened
1 cup smooth peanut butter
¼ cup half-and-half
1 teaspoon vanilla

Preheat oven to 350 degrees. Line 12 jumbo muffin tins with cupcake liners or spray with cooking spray. In a large bowl, sift together flour, baking soda, baking powder, and salt. In a separate bowl, cream together Crisco® and sugar with electric mixer until light and fluffy.

Add eggs one at a time. Then add mashed bananas. Add vanilla and mix until well combined. With mixer on low speed, add dry ingredients to wet, alternating with buttermilk and mixing well between each. Fill cupcake liners ¾ full. Bake for 45 minutes or until toothpick inserted comes out clean. Cool completely.

For the frosting, in a medium bowl mix sugar, butter, peanut butter, vanilla, and half-and-half with an electric mixer, until smooth. Frost cooled cupcakes.

Makes 12 cupcakes.

Chocolate Cupcakes with Chocolate Buttercream Icing

For all chocolate lovers: enjoy these fudgy, rich chocolate cupcakes with a cold glass of milk. They are easy to make and will please a crowd.

CAKE
1¾ cups flour
1¼ teaspoon baking soda
A pinch of salt
¾ cup butter
⅔ cup white sugar
⅔ cup brown sugar
1 cup cocoa powder
2 eggs
1½ teaspoon vanilla
1½ cup buttermilk

FROSTING
½ cup unsalted butter
2 cups powdered sugar
3 ounces unsweetened chocolate, melted
2 teaspoons vanilla
2 tablespoons cream

Preheat oven to 350 degrees. Line 12 jumbo muffin tins with cupcake liners or spray with cooking spray. In a large bowl, sift together flour, baking soda, and salt. In a separate bowl, cream together butter and sugars with electric mixer until light and fluffy. With mixer on low, slowly add cocoa powder. Then add eggs one at a time. Add vanilla. Mix until well combined.

With mixer on low speed, add dry ingredients to wet alternating with buttermilk and mixing well between each. Fill cupcake liner ¾ full. Bake for 25 minutes or until toothpick inserted comes out clean. Cool completely.

For the frosting, in a medium bowl mix sugar, butter, chocolate, cream, and vanilla with an electric mixer, until smooth. Frost cooled cupcakes.

Makes 12 cupcakes.

Chocolate Cherry Cake with Chocolate Buttercream Frosting

What better way to enjoy Door County's famous cherries than with a piece of this deliciously decadent chocolate cherry cake. You are going to love this one. Peak cherry season is late July.

CAKE
2 cups flour
1 teaspoon baking soda
A pinch of salt
½ cup unsalted butter, softened
2 cups white sugar
2 oz. bittersweet chocolate, melted
1½ cups sour cream
3 eggs
1 teaspoon vanilla
¼ cup cherry juice
1 cup cherries, pitted and finely
  chopped
½ cup walnuts, finely chopped

FROSTING
1 cup unsalted butter, softened
2 oz. unsweetened chocolate,
  melted
1 tablespoon cream
1 teaspoon vanilla
2 cups powdered sugar

Preheat oven to 350 degrees. Grease and flour two 9-inch round baking pans. In a large bowl, sift together flour, baking soda, and salt. In a separate bowl, cream together butter and sugar with electric mixer until light and fluffy. Mix in melted chocolate and sour cream. Add eggs one at a time. Add vanilla. Mix until well combined.

With mixer on low speed, add dry ingredients to wet. Add cherry juice, cherries, and nuts. Mix until combined. Pour into prepared pans and bake for 50 minutes, or until toothpick inserted comes out clean. Cool completely.

For the frosting, in a medium bowl, combine butter, chocolate, cream, and vanilla with an electric mixer. Add powdered sugar and mix until smooth. Frost cooled cake.

Jenny's Old-Fashioned Coffee Cake

I loved my grandmother's baking. Her old-fashioned coffee cake was wonderful—it just melted in your mouth. Perfect for those crisp winter afternoons with a cup of hot tea.

RICH ROLL DOUGH
1 2 oz. package cake yeast
¼ cup lukewarm water
½ cup sugar
1 teaspoon salt
¾ cup milk
2 eggs, beaten
1 teaspoon grated lemon zest
4 cups sifted flour
½ teaspoon ground cardamon
½ cup butter, melted

TOPPING
⅔ cup light brown sugar
¼ cup flour
2 teaspoons cinnamon
A pinch of salt
¼ cup butter, softened
⅔ cup chopped pecans

In a small bowl, combine lukewarm water with ½ teaspoon of sugar. Add yeast. Set aside until softened. In a small saucepan, scald milk. Add remaining sugar and salt. Stir and cool to lukewarm. Combine softened yeast with cooled milk mixture in a large bowl and stir well. Add eggs, lemon zest, half the flour, and cardamom. Beat until smooth. Beat in melted butter, then add remaining flour mixture and mix thoroughly. Place dough on a lightly floured surface, cover with a clean kitchen towel, and let rest 10 minutes. Knead until smooth and elastic, about 10 minutes, using no more than ¼ cup flour for kneading. *Secret:* do not add extra flour on the board. Sweet dough must be soft; too much flour makes the dough "bready." Ball up dough and place in a greased bowl. Turn once bring the greased side up. Preheat oven to 350 degrees for 2 minutes, then shut off. Cover dough with a towel and let rise in warm oven until double in size, about 1 hour.

Preheat oven to 400 degrees. Grease two 7x11-inch pans. Turn dough out onto lightly floured surface. Divide into two portions. Put each into a bowl and let rise 10 minutes. Roll out each portion to fit a rectangular baking 7x11-inch pan. Fit dough into greased pans and cover. Let rise in a warm place until double in size, about 1 hour. Meanwhile, make topping. Mix sugar, flour, cinnamon, and salt together. Work in soft butter to produce a coarse, crumbly mixture. Stir in nuts. Sprinkle mixture over unbaked coffee cake. Bake for 15 minutes, then reduce heat to 350 degrees and bake 15 minutes longer. Serve warm, and enjoy!

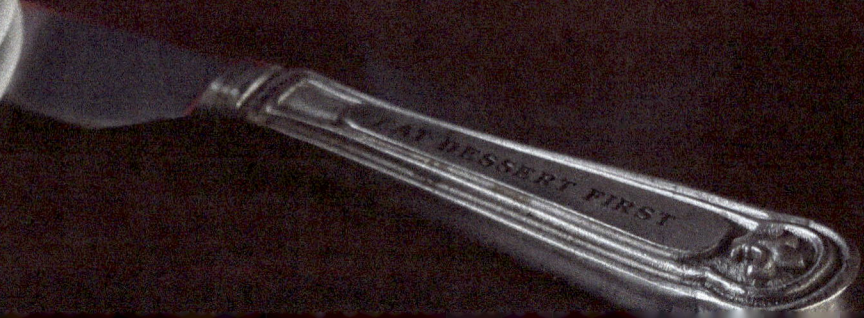

German Chocolate Cake

This was my husband Don's favorite cake. My mother or I would make it for his birthday every year. It's a little fussy. Like most men, he thought he was worth it—and he was.

CAKE
4 oz. German sweet chocolate
½ cup water
2 cups flour
1 teaspoon baking soda
A pinch of salt
4 eggs, separated
1 cup butter, softened
2 cups sugar
1 teaspoon vanilla
1 cup buttermilk

COCONUT PECAN FROSTING
4 egg yolks
1 can evaporated milk
1½ tablespoon vanilla
1½ cups sugar
¾ cup butter
14 oz. package angel flake coconut
1½ cups chopped pecans

Preheat oven to 350 degrees. Cover the bottom of three 9-inch pans with parchment paper and spray with cooking spray. Microwave chocolate and water for about 1 to 2 minutes, then stir until chocolate is melted. In a large bowl, sift together flour, baking soda, and salt. Set aside. Beat egg whites in a small bowl with mixer on high until peaks form. Set aside. Beat butter and sugar in a large bowl with mixer until light and fluffy. Add 1 egg yolk at a time, beating well after each. Blend in chocolate and vanilla.

With mixer on low speed, add flour mixture alternately with buttermilk, beating well. Fold in egg whites. Pour into pans. Bake 30 minutes or until toothpick comes out clean. Run spatula around cake pans to loosen cake, but continue to cool cakes in pans for 15 minutes. Remove cakes from pans to wire racks and cool completely.

Beat yolks, evaporated milk, and vanilla in large saucepan with whisk until blended. Add sugar and butter. Cook on medium heat about 12 minutes or until thickened and brown, stirring constantly. Remove from heat. Stir in coconut and nuts. Let frosting cool. Spread between layers and frost the cake.

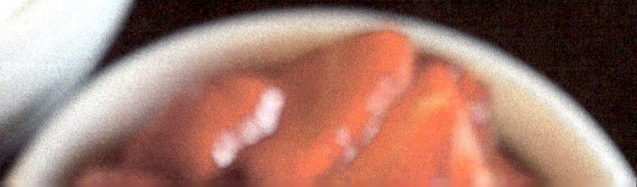

Hot Milk Cake with Strawberries and Whipped Cream

This a summer favorite one that my sons loved, especially Wayne. Perfect for a Father's Day get-together or a 4th of July picnic. The very best of summer.

CAKE
2 cups flour
2 teaspoons baking powder
4 eggs
2 cups sugar
1 teaspoon vanilla
2 cup boiling milk
2 tablespoons butter
1 quart strawberries
⅓ cup sugar (for strawberries)
Whipped cream (for serving)

Preheat oven to 350 degrees. Grease and flour a Bundt pan or 13x9-inch pan. In a large bowl, sift together flour and baking powder. In a separate large bowl, beat eggs on high speed for 5 minutes or until thick and lemon-colored. Gradually add sugar, beating until mixture is light and fluffy. Beat in vanilla. Add flour mixture to egg mixture and beat on low speed until smooth. In a small saucepan, heat milk and butter until butter is melted. Gradually add to batter. Beat until combined.

Pour into prepared pan and bake for 50 to 60 minutes for Bundt pan and 30 to 35 minutes for 13x9-inch pan or until a toothpick inserted near the center comes out clean. For Bundt pan, cool cake in the pan for 10 minutes, then invert onto a cooling rack or serving plate to cool completely.

To serve, wash and slice strawberries (Door County berries, of course). Sprinkle with ⅓ cup sugar. Let stand for 10 minutes. Cut cake and serve with a heaping spoon full of strawberries and a dollop of whipped cream.

Cookies

Chocolate Chip Cookies

This is my mother Alice's recipe, a favorite of family & friends. My three sons loved Grandma Alice's cookies. I tried and failed many times to make them—I wanted to make them on my own. Finally, I asked my mother to show me her secrets. They have also helped me pay for things, like snowplowing and repairing broken lawnmowers. My future snowplow driver, Blake (who is 5 at this writing) calls me the "Cookie Fairy" because of those magically delicious cookies!

———————————————————

2½ cups flour
1 teaspoon baking soda
A pinch of salt
1 cup Crisco®
½ cup white sugar
1¼ cup brown sugar
2 eggs
2 teaspoons vanilla
2 cups chocolate chips

Preheat oven to 300 degrees. Line two cookie sheets with parchment paper. In a large bowl, sift together flour, baking soda, and salt. In a stand mixer on medium high speed, cream together Crisco® and white sugar until light and fluffy and peaks form, about 15 to 20 minutes. Add brown sugar and mix until combined. Beat in eggs one at a time, then beat in vanilla. With mixer on low speed, gradually add flour mixture until well combined. Stir in chocolate chips.

Using an ice cream scoop, drop dough onto prepared cookie sheet 2 inches apart. Bake for 12 minutes. Let cool on cookie sheet for 10 minutes. Transfer to wire rack to cool completely.

Makes approx. 18 cookies, depending on size.

Christmas Sugar Cookies

I make approximately 350 of these cookies each Christmas. They are part of the family's Christmas presents. Grandson David also gets some for his birthday— they're his favorite.

COOKIE DOUGH
4 cups of flour
1 teaspoon baking soda
A pinch of salt
1 cup lard
2 cups white sugar
2 eggs
1½ cup sour cream
1 tablespoon vanilla
Nutmeg

FROSTING
1½ cup butter
2 cups of powdered sugar
2 tablespoon cream
1 tablespoon vanilla

Preheat oven to 350 degrees. Line 2 cookie sheets with parchment paper. In a large bowl, sift together flour, baking soda, and salt. In a stand mixer fitted with a paddle, cream lard and sugar for 20 minutes. Add eggs one at a time, mixing well between each. Add sour cream and vanilla, mixing on low speed until combined. With mixer on low speed, gradually add flour mixture until well combined. Turn dough out onto plastic wrap, sprinkle with nutmeg, wrap tightly with plastic wrap, and refrigerate overnight.

Roll dough out about ¼-inch thick on floured surface. Cut out and transfer to parchment-lined cookie sheet. Bake until light brown, about 12 minutes. Cool completely and frost.

For the frosting, on medium speed, beat butter, sugar, cream, and vanilla until smooth. Add food coloring if desired. Spread a thin coat of frosting on cooled cookies and decorate.

This recipe makes about 36 cookies, depending on cookie size.

Grandma Jenny's Kolache

This is a special treat I make for the holidays, perfect for Christmas morning with a cup of tea. These are really amazing—you can't just eat one. They can be made with a variety of fillings.

KOLACHE
1 2-oz. cake yeast
¼ cup lukewarm water
1 teaspoon sugar
¾ cup milk
¼ cup butter
¼ cup sugar
½ teaspoon salt
1 egg yolk
½ teaspoon grated lemon zest
3 cups all-purpose flour

PRUNE FILLING
½ lbs. prunes (pitted)
¼ cup sugar
¾ cup water
½ teaspoon grated lemon zest
¼ teaspoon ground cloves
¼ teaspoon allspice

In a small bowl, dissolve yeast in the lukewarm water with 1 teaspoon sugar. In a small saucepan, scald the milk and cool to lukewarm. In a large bowl, cream butter and sugar. Add salt, egg yolk, and zest. Beat until smooth. Stir in softened yeast mixture. Add flour and cooled milk alternately, stirring between each addition. Ball up dough and place in a greased bowl, turning once to bring up greased side. Cover with a clean kitchen towel. Preheat oven to 350 degrees for 5 minutes to warm up and then turn off. Place dough in warm oven to rise for about 1 hour until double in size.

Preheat oven to 350 degrees. Put dough on a floured surface and roll out about ¼ inch thick. Cut out with a round biscuit cutter and put on parchment paper on a large cookie sheet. Make wide, deep indentations in center and fill with filling. Let rise 15 minutes and bake for 15 to 20 minutes. Transfer to a cooling rack and sprinkle with powdered sugar while warm. Kolache are best eaten on the same day they are made, but can be stored in an airtight container at room temperature for up to 2 days or in the freezer for up to 3 months.

For the filling, bring to a boil in medium saucepan, prunes, sugar, and water. Simmer for 30 to 45 minutes until prunes are soft. Cool, drain juice, and reserve. Puree prunes in food processor. Add cloves and allspice. Add reserved prune juice if puree is too thick. Allow to cool before spooning into dough. Filling can be made up to five days ahead and stored in the refrigerator. You can also use pie filling. Makes 24 kolache.

Molasses Cookies

This is Grandma Jenny's recipe—and her cookie cutter. These cookies are so delicious, you cannot eat just one. I can remember both my grandmother and my mother making these. They always wore aprons back then, touched with flour and other great flavors. I can see them both in the kitchen, rolling out the dough. The smell of the cookies fresh out of the oven is like no other. Such good memories.

---

5 cups flour, plus more to make dough soft
1 teaspoon nutmeg
1 teaspoon powdered ginger
¼ teaspoon salt
1 cup sugar
1 cup lard
¼ cup boiling coffee
3 teaspoons baking soda
1 cup molasses
3 eggs, beaten

Preheat oven to 350 degrees. Line cookie sheets with parchment paper. In a large bowl, sift together flour, nutmeg, ginger, and salt. Set aside. In a separate large bowl, cream together sugar and lard. In a small bowl, dissolve baking soda in boiling coffee. Add coffee mixture and molasses to creamed sugar mixture. Add eggs and mix well. Gradually add dry ingredients stir until combined.

On a floured surface, roll out dough to ¼-inch thickness. Cut out cookies using a 4-inch or 5-inch round cookie cutter and place on lined cookie sheet. Bake for 8 minutes. Do not over-bake. Let the cookies rest on cookie sheet for 10 minutes, then remove to a wire rack.

A great treat for a snowy day or any day. These also make great ice cream sandwiches.

Makes about 24 cookies, depending on size.

Oatmeal Crispies

The smell of these baking when I came home from school was amazing. Back then, I walked home from school. Three miles on the dirt roads; even with a bike, it was hard. So, getting home and having of these cookies and a glass of milk was really special. I guess you could say my mother was awesome.

---

4 cups flour
2 teaspoon baking soda
1 teaspoon cinnamon
1 teaspoon allspice
½ teaspoon ground cloves
A pinch of salt
1 cup butter, softened
⅔ cup shortening
⅔ cup white sugar
⅔ cup brown sugar
4 eggs
2 teaspoons vanilla
2 cups quick cooking oats
1 cup chopped pecans
1½ cups dried cherries

Preheat oven to 375 degrees. Grease cookie sheets. In a large bowl, combine flour, baking soda, spices and salt. Set aside. In a large mixing bowl on medium speed, cream together butter, shortening, and sugar. Beat in eggs one at a time. Stir in vanilla. On low speed, gradually add in flour mixture. Stir in oats, nuts, and dried cherries.

Drop by small ice cream scoop onto a greased cookie sheet. Bake for 10 minutes. Remove from oven and cool on cookie sheets for two minutes, then cool completely on wire racks.

Makes about 18 cookies, depending on size.

Peanut Butter Cookies

These are a favorite of everyone I work with. There is always a fight to make sure they are evenly distributed. Some people hide a few; one can't wait to get home and eats hers on the way. Some say they aren't going to have any and end up eating the most. One of them breaks hers into pieces and freezes the rest. This one is for you, Danelle.

2½ cups flour
1 teaspoon baking soda
A pinch of salt
1 cup butter, softened
1 cup creamy peanut butter
1 cup white sugar
1 cup brown sugar
2 eggs
1 teaspoon vanilla

Preheat oven to 300 degrees. In a large bowl, combine flour, baking soda, and salt and set aside. In a large mixing bowl on medium speed, cream together butter, peanut butter, and sugars. Beat in eggs one at a time. Stir in vanilla. On low speed, gradually add in flour mixture.

Refrigerate dough overnight. Using an ice cream scoop, roll dough into balls and place them on cookie sheet 2 inches apart. Using a fork, flatten cookies in a criss-cross pattern.

Bake 12 minutes, just until they puff up. Don't over-bake. They will flatten out as they set. That's what gives them that chewy texture.

Makes about 18 cookies, depending on size.

Pecan Cookies

These are incredible! I usually bake 4 double batches of them at Christmas. Everyone looks forward to getting a special delivery of these sweet treats. My family loves them and yours will, too.

———————————————————

1 cup butter
4 tablespoons powdered sugar
1 tablespoon ice water
2 cups flour
1 cup chopped pecans
1 tablespoon vanilla extract
3 cups powdered sugar

Preheat oven to 250 degrees. Line cookie sheet with parchment paper. In a food processor, pulse butter, powdered sugar, and water, until creamy. Add flour and pulse until well mixed. Add pecans and vanilla, pulse until combined.

Using your hands, roll dough into 2-inch logs. I use plastic gloves that I keep wet, which helps with the stickiness. Place logs on parchment lined cookie sheet and bake for one hour. Let cool and roll in powdered sugar.

Makes about 36 cookies, depending on size.

Other Sweets

Banana Bread

This is one of the family's big favorites, especially my great-granddaughter Brynn, who loves it with strawberry jam. The secret for this recipe is to freeze ripe bananas and thaw them when you're ready to bake.

---

2 cups flour
1 teaspoon baking soda
A pinch of salt
½ cup Crisco®
1 cup brown sugar
2 ripe bananas, mashed or frozen and thawed
2 eggs
½ cup buttermilk

Preheat oven to 350 degrees. Lightly grease a 9x5-inch loaf pan.
In a large bowl, sift flour, baking soda, and salt. Set aside.

In a separate bowl, cream together Crisco® and brown sugar. Add mashed bananas. Mix well. Add eggs one at a time mix until well combined.
Add flour mixture a little at a time, alternating with buttermilk.
Stir until combined.

Bake for one hour, until a toothpick inserted into center of the loaf comes out clean. Let bread cool in pan for 10 minutes, then turn out onto a wire rack.

Cinnamon Rolls

This recipe was adapted from my grandmother's coffee cake recipe. They can be made when you have a little extra time then pop them in the freezer, and heat them up when needed.

RICH ROLL DOUGH
1 2 oz. cake yeast
¼ cup lukewarm water
½ cup sugar
1 teaspoon salt
¾ cup milk
2 eggs, beaten
1 teaspoon grated lemon zest
4 cups sifted flour
½ teaspoon ground cardamom
½ cup butter, melted

FILLING
¼ cup butter, softened
1 teaspoon cinnamon
¼ cup sugar
½ cup pecans, chopped

GLAZE
1½ cups powdered sugar
¼ cup butter
1 teaspoon vanilla
3 tablespoons half-and-half

In a small bowl, combine lukewarm water with ½ tsp sugar. Add yeast. Set aside until softened. In a small saucepan, scald milk. Add remaining sugar and salt. Stir and cool to lukewarm. Combine softened yeast with cooled milk mixture in a large bowl and stir well. Add eggs, lemon zest, half the flour, and cardamom. Beat until smooth. Beat in melted butter, then add remaining flour mixture and stir thoroughly. Place dough on a lightly floured surface. Cover with a clean kitchen towel and let rest 10 minutes. Knead until smooth and elastic, about 10 minutes using no more than ¼ cup flour for kneading. *Secret*: Do not add extra flour on the board. Sweet dough must be soft; too much flour make the dough "bready." Ball up dough and place in a greased bowl. Turn once bring the greased side up. Preheat oven to 350 degrees for 2 minutes then shut off. Cover dough with a towel and let rise in warm oven until double in size, about 1 hour.

Preheat oven to 350 degrees. On a floured surface, roll out dough to a 15x8-inch rectangle about ⅜-inch thick. Spread softened butter over dough. Combine cinnamon, sugar, and pecans and sprinkle onto dough. Roll up like a jelly roll. Seal edge, turn seal underneath, and cut to make 6 rolls. Put cut side up into a large muffin pan. Bake for 25 minutes. While cinnamon rolls are baking, prepare glaze. In a medium bowl using a hand mixer, whip butter until light and fluffy. Slowly mix in powdered sugar, vanilla, and half-and-half. Remove rolls from oven and glaze.

Makes 6 rolls.

Cream Puffs

This recipe was always a Father's Day treat. They are not as hard to make as you might think and are always a delicious surprise any time of year.

CREAM PUFFS
½ cup water
¼ cup butter
⅛ teaspoon salt
½ cup white flour
2 eggs

FILLING
1 cup heavy whipping cream
¼ cup sugar
1 tablespoon vanilla
½ cup powdered sugar

Preheat oven to 350 degrees. Line baking sheet with parchment paper. In a medium saucepan, bring water, butter, and salt to a boil. Add flour all at once and beat over low heat until mixture leaves the side of the pan and forms a ball. Remove from heat and continue beating to cool down dough, about 2 minutes. Add one egg at a time, beating well after each egg. Continue to beat until mixture has a satin-like sheen.

Drop ¼-cup mounds of batter, swirling the top of each, onto parchment-lined pans. Bake for about 50 min or until they turn brown and puff up. Remove from oven and cut 1 or 2 slits on each side. Return to oven for 10 minutes. Cool on a wire rack.

For filling, beat heavy cream with sugar and vanilla until stiff peaks form. Cut tops off puffs and fill with cream. Return tops and dust with powdered sugar.

Makes 6 cream puffs.

Don's Chocolate Fudge

My husband, Don, made fudge at Christmas for the family. He wasn't much of a baker, but this recipe is not too difficult and he was very proud of it. We miss him and his fudge.

---

3 cups semi-sweet chocolate chips
1 14 oz. can sweetened condensed milk
A pinch of salt
1 cup chopped walnuts
1½ teaspoon vanilla

Line an 8x8-inch pan with aluminum foil. In a heavy saucepan over low heat, melt chocolate chips with sweetened condensed milk and a pinch of salt. Stir until smooth. Remove from heat. Stir in walnuts and vanilla.

Spread evenly into a foil-lined pan. Chill in the refrigerator for 2 hours or until firm. Turn fudge onto a cutting board, peel off foil and cut into squares. Store loosely covered at room temperature.

Pecan Tartlets

These are a delicious special treat. Enjoy and remember a good dose of love goes into them.

½ cup butter, softened
½ cup sugar
2 egg yolks
1 teaspoon almond extract
2 cups flour, sifted
⅓ cup dark corn syrup
1 cup powdered sugar
1 cup chopped pecans

Preheat oven to 400 degrees. Cream together butter and sugar. Add egg yolks and almond extract. Mix until combined. Gradually add flour and mix until coarse and crumbly.

Press 1 tablespoon of dough evenly into mini muffin tins. Bake for 8 to 10 minutes, until lightly browned. (Leave oven on.) Remove from oven and cool on wire rack. In a medium saucepan, on medium-low heat, bring to a boil dark corn syrup and powdered sugar. Stir occasionally for 4 to 5 minutes or until mixture comes to a full boil. Remove from heat. Stir in chopped pecans.

Spoon pecan mixture into shells, and bake for 5 minutes.

Makes 24 tartlets.

Pumpkin Bread

This is a great fall treat, when the air is crisp and the leaves start to turn. That's also a great time to visit Door County, when the summer has come to a close and there's a calm, cozy feeling in the county.

---

2 cups flour
1 teaspoon salt
¼ teaspoon baking powder
½ teaspoon baking soda
1 teaspoon cinnamon
1 teaspoon ground nutmeg
½ teaspoon ground ginger
1 cup brown sugar, firmly packed
½ cup white sugar
1 cup pumpkin
½ cup olive oil
2 eggs
1 cup dried cherries or cranberries
½ chopped walnuts

Preheat oven to 350 degrees. Grease and flour loaf pan. In a medium bowl, whisk together flour, salt, baking powder, baking soda, and spices. Set aside.

In a large bowl, beat sugars, pumpkin, oil, and eggs until well combined. Slowly stir in flour mixture. Stir in cherries and walnuts.

Pour into prepared loaf pan. Bake for 1 hour and 10 minutes, or until a toothpick inserted into center of loaf comes out clean. Let cool in pan for 10 minutes. Remove bread from pan and cool completely on wire rack.

Mother's Rice Pudding

I loved this as a child, and so did my sons. Picture cozying up with a warm serving of rice pudding on a snowy winter day. Yummy! This reminds me, I need to treat myself, even if it's not a snow day.

---

1 cup white rice
2 cups whole milk
¼ cup sugar
Pinch of cinnamon
1 tablespoon butter

In a double boiler, combine rice, milk, and sugar. Bring to a boil, then reduce to a simmer for one hour, stirring frequently. As the mixture thickens, add extra milk as needed. Cook until nice and creamy. Stir in raisins if desired.

Pour into a small bowl add butter and sprinkle with cinnamon.

Strawberry Jam

This jam goes so well with banana bread! My son John and great- granddaughters Brynn and Adelaide love it. Of course, you must start with Door County strawberries. This sweet treat is so easy and so good, I can't wait until strawberry season.

2 cups fresh strawberries, crushed
4 cups sugar
2 tablespoon lemon juice
½ bottle liquid Certo®

In a large bowl, thoroughly mix strawberries and sugar. Let stand 10 minutes. In a small bowl, mix lemon juice with Certo® and add to berries. Stir for 3 minutes. Pour into 8 oz. jars let stand for 24 hours, then refrigerate or freeze.

Pies

Pie Crust

My sister-in-law Shirley always wanted me to send her just the crust. She could never figure out how I could make it so thin and flaky. I always brought a fresh pie when I went to visit her. After lunch, we always had pie.

_____

SINGLE PIE CRUST
1 cup flour
¼ cup lard
A pinch of salt
Approximately 4 tablespoons ice water

DOUBLE PIE CRUST
1½ cups flour
½ cup lard
A pinch of salt
Approximately 6 tablespoons of ice water

In a medium bowl, work the lard into the flour until it is pea-sized and crumbles. Add ice water 1 tablespoon at a time until the dough holds together in a ball. Place on a floured surface. Roll out and turn, rolling until it is the desired thickness.

Alice's Old-fashioned Banana Cream Pie

This was my mother's favorite pie. Once you taste it, you will agree. Thanks, Mom, for this and all the other great recipes.

Single pie crust (p. 55)

1 ripe banana
3 cups whole milk
¾ cup white sugar
⅓ cup flour
A pinch of salt
3 egg yolks, lightly beaten
2 tablespoons butter
1 cup heavy cream
¼ cup sugar
1 tablespoon vanilla

Preheat oven to 350 degrees. Prepare single pie crust. Roll out and place in pie dish. Bake with weights for 10 minutes or golden brown. Let cool completely.

Place sliced banana on the bottom of pie crust. In a medium saucepan, scald milk and set aside. In a heavy saucepan, put sugar, flour, and salt. Stir in milk. Place over medium heat, stirring until the mixture thickens, about 2 minutes. Stir in egg yolks and cook another minute. Add butter and vanilla.

Pour into pie crust and cover with plastic wrap. Let chill for 2 hours.

Before serving, in a medium bowl, whip cream until soft peaks form. Mix in sugar and vanilla. Top pie with whipped cream and serve.

Blackberry Pecan Streusel Pie

This is a really easy and tasty treat when berry season is in full swing. There's nothing like picking your own berries for this recipe if you're lucky enough to have a blackberry bush in the backyard.

Single pie crust (p. 55)

FILLING
4 cups blackberries
1 cup sugar
½ cup quick-cooking tapioca
1 teaspoon cinnamon

STREUSEL TOPPING
½ cup flour
¼ cup sugar
¼ cup cold butter
¼ cup chopped pecans

Preheat oven to 375 degrees. Prepare a single pie crust.

In a medium saucepan, combine blackberries, sugar, tapioca, and cinnamon. Bring to a boil over medium heat. Reduce heat and simmer for 10 minutes, stirring often. Remove from heat to cool.

Meanwhile, prepare streusel topping. In a medium bowl, combine flour, sugar, and butter until it forms pea-sized crumbles. Stir in pecans.

Pour filling into pie crust and top with pecan streusel. Bake for 25 minutes until crust is golden brown.

Blueberry Pie

Nothing beats a slice of blueberry pie topped with a scoop of vanilla ice cream at the end of a delicious meal.

Double pie crust (p. 55)

4 cups blueberries
1 cup sugar
¼ cup quick cooking tapioca
1 tablespoon lemon juice
⅛ teaspoon cinnamon
1 tablespoon butter
2 tablespoons sugar for sprinkling on top

Preheat oven to 400 degrees. Prepare double pie crusts.

In a medium bowl, combine blueberries, sugar, tapioca, lemon juice, and cinnamon. Let stand for 15 minutes. Fill lower pie crust with blueberry mixture, then dot with butter. Seal and cut several slits in the top crust for steam to escape. Sprinkle crust with white sugar.

Bake for 45 to 50 minutes, until crust is golden brown. Remove from oven and cool on a wire rack.

Cherry Pie

Door County is known for its cherries. They are simply the best—sweet and tart and delicious. This pie is wonderful with a scoop of vanilla ice cream.

Double pie crust (p. 55)

4 cups pitted sour cherries, from Door County, of course!
1 ½ cup sugar
3 tablespoons quick cooking tapioca
¼ teaspoon almond extract
1 tablespoon butter
2 tablespoons sugar for sprinkling on top

Preheat oven to 400 degrees. Prepare double pie crusts.

In a large bowl, mix cherries with sugar, tapioca, and almond extract. Let stand for 15 minutes.

Roll out lower pie crust and place in pie tin. Fill with cherry mixture and dot with butter. Roll out second crust. Crimp edges of crust and cut several slits in the top to permit steam to escape. Sprinkle top with sugar.

Bake for 45 to 50 minutes until crust is golden brown. Cool on wire rack.

Chocolate Pudding Pie

My love for chocolate includes this extra-delicious chocolate pie. I haven't made it lately, but just looking at the recipe reminds me of its mouth-watering taste. Time to make it again!

CRUST
30 chocolate wafers or graham crackers
3 oz. bittersweet chocolate, melted
1 tablespoon canola oil

FILLING
¾ cup sugar
¼ cup cornstarch
¼ cup unsweetened cocoa
A pinch of salt
1¾ cup 2% milk
2 large egg yolks
4 oz. bittersweet chocolate, finely chopped
1 teaspoon vanilla

Place wafers or graham crackers in food processor and process until finely ground. Add melted chocolate and oil. Press into 9-inch pie plate.

In a large saucepan, combine sugar, cornstarch, cocoa, and salt. Stir with a whisk. Add half of the milk and 2 egg yolks. Stir with whisk until smooth. Stir in remaining milk. Cook over medium heat for about 5 minutes, or until thick and bubbling. Add chopped chocolate and stir until smooth. Stir in vanilla.

Pour mixture into crust. Cover with plastic wrap and chill for 4 hours. Serve with fresh raspberries and whipped cream. Just the best ever!

Lemon Cream Pie

Like my granddaughter-in-law (and photographer of this book) Sandy says, "Yum!" This is a great dessert if you're planning a heavy meal like the Country Ribs and Potato Dumplings (p. 83). It's light, sweet, a little tart, and easy to make a day ahead.

Single pie crust (p. 55)

½ cup sugar
1 tablespoon grated lemon zest
¼ cup lemon juice
3 tablespoons cornstarch
A pinch of salt
2 large eggs
1½ cup whole milk
2 ounces cream cheese, softened
2 tablespoons butter, softened
1 cup heavy cream

Preheat oven to 400 degrees. Prepare pie crust. Bake with pie weights until golden brown, 12 to 15 minutes. Cool on wire rack.

In a large bowl combine sugar, lemon zest, lemon juice, cornstarch, salt, and eggs. In a medium saucepan over medium heat, mix milk and cream cheese together. Heat until tiny bubbles form around the edges. Gradually add milk mixture to lemon mixture, stirring with a whisk until combined. Return to saucepan and cook over medium heat about 10 minutes, or until bubbly, stirring constantly. Remove from heat and stir in butter. Place pan in large ice-filled bowl for about 10 minutes or until it cools, stirring constantly.

Spoon into crust and cover with plastic wrap. Chill for 3 hours. Whip cream until soft peaks form. Spread over pie and serve.

Apple Pie Cuts

These are just yummy. My mother made these for Sunday dinner as a special treat. They are a little difficult to make and I have thrown away the dough, and started over a few times before finding the secret of chilling the dough and using a Silpat non-stick baking mat for rolling it out. They are worth the extra time. Enjoy and remember they are made special—you'll feel special eating them.

DOUGH
¾ cup butter,
   softened
¼ cup sugar
¼ lemon juice
2½ cups flour
1 tablespoon vanilla

FILLING
7 Macintosh apples,
   peeled and thinly
   sliced
1 tablespoon apple pie
   spice
1 tablespoon cinnamon
¼ cup sugar

FROSTING
½ cup butter, softened
1½ cup powdered sugar
1 tablespoon vanilla

In a large bowl, cream together butter and sugar. Add lemon juice, and slowly add flour. Mix in vanilla. Wrap dough in plastic wrap and chill dough in refrigerator for 1 hour.

Preheat oven to 350 degrees. Spray two 14x4.5-inch tart pans with cooking spray. Cut dough in half, storing the remainder in the refrigerator. Cut dough in half again and roll out on a lightly floured Silpat non-stick baking mat until dough extends over the edge of the tart pan by an inch or two. Place dough in pans.

Peel and slice apples directly into tart pan. Sprinkle with apple pie spice, cinnamon, and sugar. Roll out remaining dough and place over apples. Fold bottom dough over top to seal. Cut 3 to 4 one-inch vent holes on top dough. Bake for 45 minutes or until brown and bubbling. Meanwhile, make frosting. In a medium bowl, beat butter and powdered sugar on low speed until combined. Mix in vanilla. Spread over pie cuts warm from the oven.

P.S. You can also use blueberries or cherries for the filling.

Makes 12 pie cuts.

Pumpkin Pie

This pie is a Thanksgiving and Christmas tradition. My grandmother Jenny made it, as did my mother Alice—and now I am handing it down to you. It's the best pumpkin pie you'll ever sink your teeth into. This recipe makes 3 pies.

---

3 single pie crusts (p. 55)

14 oz. can of pumpkin filling
3 tbsp flour
1 cup brown sugar
1 cup white sugar
A pinch of salt
2 teaspoon pumpkin pie spice
1 teaspoon ginger
1 teaspoon cinnamon
14 oz can of condensed milk
6 eggs
3 cups whole milk

Preheat oven to 350 degrees. Prepare pie crusts. Bake with pie weights until golden brown, 12 to 15 minutes. Cool on wire rack.

In a large bowl, mix together pumpkin, flour, sugars, salt, and spices until well combined. Mix in condensed milk and eggs. In a medium saucepan, bring milk to a boil. Remove from heat and pour slowly into pumpkin mixture. Beat until smooth.

Pour into prepared pie crusts. Bake for approximately 1 hour or until a knife comes out clean when inserted in the middle. Cool on a wire rack.

Whip cream until soft peaks form. Serve each slice with a dollop of whipped cream.

Savory Dishes

Asparagus and Smoked Salmon Tart

This is one of my favorite recipes. I created it out of my love for smoked salmon and asparagus. It's a great dish for brunch or a wonderful meal paired with a salad.

---

1 sheet frozen puff pastry, thawed
1 tablespoon olive oil
1 medium onion, chopped
Salt and pepper to taste
2 eggs
½ cup sour cream
1 teaspoon dried dill
4 oz smoked salmon
16 thin asparagus stalks, woody ends removed
½ cup shredded Italian cheese blend

Preheat oven to 350 degrees. Grease or spray with cooking spray two tart pans with removable bottoms. Unfold puff pastry, cut to fit, and press into tart pans.

In a large skillet over medium heat sauté onion in oil for about 4 minutes. Remove from heat and let cool slightly. Season with salt and pepper.

In a medium bowl, whisk the eggs, sour cream, and dill until well blended. Mix in chopped onion. Cut or break up salmon into bite-sized pieces and add to egg mixture, gently mixing to combine.

Pour mixture into prepared pans and arrange asparagus on top. Bake for approximately an hour or until the filling is set. Then sprinkle cheese on top and let sit in the oven until it melts.

Chicken and Broccoli Casserole

This is a tasty dinner that is easy to make on those busy weeknights. It's great served with rice or mashed potatoes. I love the difference the mayonnaise and curry powder makes in the flavor of the chicken.

———————————————————

4 skinless, boneless chicken breasts
1 head of broccoli, cut into bite-sized pieces
1 cup Greek yogurt
1 cup mayonnaise
1 teaspoon curry powder
1 cup grated cheddar cheese
1 cup bread crumbs
1 teaspoon paprika

Preheat oven to 350 degrees.

Spread broccoli in an even layer at the bottom of a 9x11-inch baking dish.

In a medium bowl, mix Greek yogurt, mayonnaise, and curry powder. Pour half the mixture over broccoli. Place chicken breasts on top and pour on remaining soup mixture. Sprinkle cheese on top, then bread crumbs and paprika.

Bake for 30 minutes, or until the internal temperature of chicken reaches 165 degrees.

Serves 4.

Chicken Pot Pies

A great dinner, especially if made ahead of time. These pies can be stored in the freezer until you are ready to serve. Then just pop them in the oven. I loved to make these when my boys were home and I was working. A nice salad and a homemade roll—boom! There's dinner.

Single pie crust (p. 55)

4 tablespoons butter
2 tablespoon heavy cream
4 tablespoons flour
2 cups chicken broth
2 red potatoes, diced and steamed
1 cup peas
3 carrots, sliced and steamed
2 cups shredded rotisserie chicken
2 tablespoons butter, melted, to brush on crust

Preheat oven to 350 degrees. Prepare pie crust.

In a medium saucepan, melt butter in heavy cream. Whisk in flour. Add chicken broth. Continue whisking until thick. Mix in vegetables and chicken.

Pour into two small 4-inch baking dishes. Roll out pie crust and divide into 2 parts. Cover baking dishes. Seal and crimp edges. Slice air holes on top. Brush with melted butter and bake for approximately 50 minutes or until bubbly and the crust is golden brown.

Serves 2 to 4, depending on appetite.

Marinated Chicken and Roasted Potatoes

This recipe is great on the grill or roasted in the oven. We always grilled out for Father's Day, with Dad's marinated chicken and potatoes. For dessert, we had yummy Cream Puffs (p. 41). The grandkids still call it "burnt chicken," depending on who did the grilling and how many Manhattans Dad had enjoyed.

CHICKEN MARINADE
4 chicken breasts
¼ cup olive oil
2 tbsp white wine vinegar
1 tbsp Dijon mustard
1 stem of rosemary

ROASTED POTATOES
2 pounds baby red potatoes, cut into bite size
1 large sweet onion, chopped
¼ cup butter
¼ cup olive oil
Salt and pepper to taste

In a small bowl, whisk olive oil, vinegar, and mustard. Put in a large Ziplock® bag, along with rosemary and chicken breast. Refrigerate for two hours.

Grill approximately 12 minutes, or until internal temperature reaches 165 degrees. Let rest 5 minutes. OR Bake in 400-degree oven for 25 minutes, or until internal temperature reaches 165 degrees. Let rest 5 minutes. Turn chicken halfway through baking.

FOR POTATOES
Combine potatoes, onion, butter, olive oil, and salt and pepper.

Put in a large sheet of aluminum foil. Fold up nice and tight. Put on the grill for 30 minutes, turning packet as you grill OR roast on a cookie sheet in a 400-degree oven for 25 minutes. Stir halfway through roasting.

Serves 4.

Country Ribs and Potato Dumplings

This recipe came from my husband Don's grandma, Edna, who was German. Don grew up eating this dish and it is a special family treat to this day. I make this for my son Jim's birthday dinner and it's also my daughter-in-law Seanna's favorite meal.

---

4 lbs country ribs
1 large can Frank's sauerkraut
4 lbs red potatoes, peeled and cut into chunks
4 eggs
Approx. 4½ cups flour
1 large white onion, sliced
½ lb. butter

COUNTRY RIBS

Preheat oven to 300 degrees. Put ribs and sauerkraut in a Dutch oven. Season with salt and pepper. Cover and cook for 5 hours. Uncover and cook another 2 hours.

DUMPLINGS

In a large stock pot, boil potatoes until tender, allow to cool, and put them through a ricer into a large bowl. Add salt and pepper to taste. Add 1 egg at a time and work into potatoes. Then add approximately 4½ cups of flour until dough comes together into a ball. In a medium frying pan over medium-low heat, sauté onion in butter until brown. Set aside.

Fill a large stock pot approx. ¾-full with water and bring to a boil. Make small ¼-cup-sized balls from the potato dough. Drop the dumplings into the water and cook until they come up to the top of the kettle, about 15 minutes. Remove dumplings with a slotted spoon and place in a large serving bowl. Pour onion butter mixture over the dumplings.

Serve the ribs and sauerkraut straight from the Dutch oven with a couple of dumplings on the side. Don't forget the rolls. Truly the best dinner for a cold winter day.

Serves 4 or more.

Cream of Broccoli Soup

My granddaughter Rachel loves this soup. It's her favorite. I always bring her this when something important happens in her life, like a job promotion. That reminds me—I need to make her some again. It reminds me of a French soup I loved.

---

3 tablespoons butter
½ cup white wine
1 medium white onion, chopped
1 cup celery, chopped
1 cup broccoli, chopped
1 cup sliced mushrooms
3 tablespoons flour
3 cups chicken broth
Salt and pepper to taste
A sprig of thyme
½ cup half & half
½ cup heavy cream

In a medium stock pot, melt butter, then add the wine. Add the vegetables and cook on low heat for about 5 minutes. Stir in flour. Add chicken broth and bring to boil for 1 minute. Add thyme, salt, and pepper and simmer for 20 minutes until the vegetables are tender. Add half-and-half and cream.

This is great served with my homemade Whole Wheat Crescent Rolls (p. 97). It makes a delicious Sunday night supper.

Serves 4.

Lasagna

Family members all agree that this dish is delicious. It's part of their Christmas care package and a birthday dinner for my son John. It takes some time for the sauce to simmer to perfection, but it's worth it.

SAUCE
1½ lb. ground chuck
1 large sweet onion, chopped
3 tablespoons olive oil
¼ cup minced garlic
1 teaspoon dried oregano
½ teaspoon pepper
1 teaspoon salt or to taste
1 28-oz. can whole tomatoes
1 28-oz. can pureed tomatoes
2 28-oz. cans tomato sauce

FOR THE LASAGNA
12 no-cook lasagna noodles
16 oz. ricotta cheese
9 large slices of mozzarella
1 lb. shredded mozzarella
2 cups 4-cheese Italian blend, shredded
1 cup Parmesan cheese, grated

In a large saucepan over medium-high heat, brown meat and onion in olive oil. Add garlic, oregano, salt, and pepper to taste. Stir until fragrant. Add the tomatoes and simmer uncovered until thick, about six hours. The long simmer time creates a well-balanced sauce with a superb texture. It's well worth the time it takes.

To assemble the lasagna, spoon a layer of sauce on the bottom of a 9x11-inch pan, then place a layer of noodles, followed by a layer of ricotta and mozzarella. Repeat layering, ending with a layer of sauce. Finish by sprinkling the Italian 4-cheese blend over the top.

Bake for 50 minutes. Let lasagna rest for 10 minutes, then sprinkle with grated Parmesan cheese. Serve with garlic bread and a salad for a dinner you'll never forget!

Serves 6.

Chunky Dill Pickles

This is a very easy recipe and so very good. A favorite of my friend, the "Pickle Queen." She made the best pickles ever. I loved her garden of cucumbers.

_____

2 lbs. cucumbers
3 stems fresh dill
½ medium onion, sliced
1 cup sugar
1 cup vinegar
1 teaspoon salt

Wash and slice cucumbers and pack in sterilized quart jar with dill and onions.

In a medium saucepan, add sugar, vinegar, and salt. Bring to a boil. Pour hot liquid over pickles and seal jar.

Place jars in hot water bath up to the neck of the jar. Boil 20 minutes or until pickles start to turn color. Take out of hot water bath and let cool. You can tell they are sealed when they pop.

This recipe is for a one-quart jar. Multiply recipe to the desired amount.

Alice's Potato Salad

A great side dish for a big summer picnic, or when grilling out at the end of a beautiful day of boating, swimming, or just relaxing here in Door County. Don't forget the beer and the brats to go with this yummy potato salad. The bowl shown here was my mother's and I always think of her when I make this salad.

---

4 lbs. baby red potatoes, boiled and peeled
Dozen eggs, hard-boiled and peeled
1 large white onion, chopped or sliced
4 cups Miracle Whip®
8 oz. container sour cream
¼ cup yellow mustard
Salt and pepper to taste
Paprika

In a large bowl, slice a layer of the cooked and peeled red potatoes. Add a layer of sliced eggs and a layer of onion. Repeat layering until all ingredients have been used. Reserve a few hard-boiled eggs for garnish.

In a separate bowl, mix the Miracle Whip®, sour cream, mustard, salt, and pepper together. Pour over layers and gently mix with two big forks until combined. Slice a few eggs for the top and sprinkle with paprika.

Serves approx. 12.

Sweet Corn Quiche

This is a wonderful quiche, especially when sweet corn is in season, and worth the effort to put up corn for those long winter months. It's also a hit at luncheons or Easter brunch. Serve with fresh fruit salad or my whole wheat crescent rolls.

Single pie crust (p. 55)

1 small pepper, chopped
1 small onion, chopped
3 tablespoons butter
4 eggs
¼ cup half-and-half
1 pound diced ham, cooked
2½ cups fresh or thawed frozen sweet corn
½ cup shredded cheddar cheese
2 dashes Worcestershire sauce
Salt and pepper to taste

Preheat oven to 350 degrees.

Prepare a single pie crust. Roll out to fit 7x11-inch baking dish.
Set aside.

In a medium frying pan, sauté onions and peppers in butter until soft.
Set aside to cool.

In a large bowl, beat eggs and cream until combined. Add onion mixture, ham, corn, cheese, salt, pepper, and Worcestershire sauce.

Pour mixture into prepared crust. Bake for 1 hour.

Serves approximately 6.

Whole Wheat Crescent Rolls

My mother made this recipe as white bread, when I was young. I changed it to whole wheat rolls 25 years ago and love them with butter or peanut butter. I bring them to all occasions, they freeze well and reheat easy. My son Jim, loves to have them on hand for Sunday dinners. For me a large salad or bowl of soup with a roll is a great dinner.

⅓ cup lard
3 cups whole milk
1 cup water
1 medium red potato peeled and finely diced
2 oz. package of cake yeast (found in the refrigerator section)
     or 3 packages of dry active yeast
2 tablespoons sugar
3 cups unbleached all-purpose flour
5 cups 50/50 flour or whole wheat flour
¼ cup butter

In medium saucepan, bring milk and lard to a low boil and set aside to cool to 90-95 degrees. Boil potato in 1 cup cold water until soft. Do not drain. Mash until smooth. In a large bowl, stir cooled milk mixture, cake yeast, and sugar, until yeast and sugar are dissolved. Add mashed potato. Then add unbleached flour and mix well.

Preheat oven to 350 degrees for 1 minute, then turn off oven. Place dough in a metal bowl in oven for 45 minutes to rise. Remove dough from oven, preheat oven to 350 degrees, and line baking sheets with parchment paper.

In a large metal bowl, add proofed dough and 50/50 flour. Mix well. Turn out onto floured surface and knead until it is squeaky, about 10 min. On floured surface, cut dough into 7 sections. Roll 1 section at a time out into 8x11-inch rectangles. Cut into 4 or 5 triangles with pizza cutter. Roll up the triangles, starting with the wide end.

Place rolls on a parchment-lined baking sheet. Brush with melted butter. Cover with towel and let rise 15 minutes. Bake for 15 minutes or until brown. Remove from oven and brush again with melted butter.

Makes 36 rolls. To freeze, allow to cool completely and store in a freezer bag. When ready to use, bake in 400-degree oven for 10 minutes.

Salmon and Wild Rice

This is my favorite Monday night dinner. It is so easy, delicious, and so good for you. Serve it with a simple kale salad on the side. Prepare it in the morning and it's ready to go in the oven when you get home from a long day at work.

Zest and juice from 1 lemon
2 tablespoons olive oil
5 to 8 oz salmon filet
¼ cup wild rice
2 cups chicken broth
2 stems of rosemary

In a small baking dish, whisk lemon zest, lemon juice, and olive oil until combined. Add salmon and turn to coat. Add stem of rosemary. Cover with plastic wrap and refrigerate for 2 to 6 hours.

Preheat oven to 300 degrees. In a separate small baking dish, combine rice, chicken broth, and stem of rosemary. Bake for an hour and a half.

Turn oven down to 175 degrees. Add baking dish with salmon to oven and bake for 20 minutes. The salmon should be just pink and flake with a fork.

This recipe serves one. Double or triple as needed.

Home for the Holidays

(The recipes shown in this section serve around 20 people.)

Roasted Turkey and Dressing

Of course, the turkey is #1, I do it a little differently. I marinade the turkey for 12 hours and cook it upside down—yes, you heard me right—with the breast down. I also cook it in a Nesco roaster—it cooks faster and stays juicy. You have my permission to flip the bird—a little humor.

Last Christmas, I had quite the experience. The knob on my Nesco broke and instead of being at 400, it was set at 200 degrees! The turkey wasn't done; my brother-in-law came to the rescue by cutting up the bird and nuking it in the microwave. I never knew one could do that. It was not as moist as my traditional cooking method, but we all survived. Twenty people, no turkey done and all the sides finished and getting cold. We learn from our experiences—it's called life!

TURKEY
20 lb. fresh turkey
1 cup sea salt
1 cup sugar
1 teaspoon salt
1 teaspoon pepper
3 teaspoons poultry seasoning
1 stick butter, melted

DRESSING
1½ bags of seasoned bread cubes
2½ lbs. lean ground beef
3 eggs
2 teaspoons poultry seasoning

Remove neck and giblets from turkey cavity. Rinse and pat turkey dry. Place turkey in a sanitized 5-gallon pail. Add sugar and salt and fill with enough water to cover. Place pail in the fridge or in a place cold enough to stay between 30 and 40 degrees for 12 hours. Remove turkey and drain. Season the cavity with salt, pepper, and poultry seasoning.

Dressing: In a large bowl, mix bread cubes, ground beef, eggs, and poultry seasoning until well combined. Stuff dressing into turkey and brush turkey with melted butter. Place turkey in roasting bag and place breast side down in Nesco roaster oven. Roast on 400 degrees for the first 2 hours, then lower the heat to 350 degrees. Cook until internal temperature reaches 165 degrees, approximately 2 hours.

Turkey Gravy

What can I say? Really the best part of any holiday meal, a splurge for sure. While you're indulging, enjoy it on your dressing as well.

---

1 cup turkey drippings
¼ cup turkey fat or butter
¼ Wondra® flour
1 cup chicken broth
Salt and pepper to taste

Remove turkey from pan. Drain all juices into a heat-proof measuring container. Allow drippings to cool and skim off fat, reserving ¼ cup.

In a medium saucepan, heat up fat and whisk flour into it until it forms a thin paste. Slowly whisk in the turkey drippings and broth. Heat and whisk until desired thickness. Add salt and pepper to taste.

Mashed Potatoes

There is nothing better than mashed potatoes with turkey gravy. It wouldn't be Christmas dinner without them.

---

10 lbs. Yukon Gold potatoes
1 stick of butter
1 cup half-and-half
Salt and pepper to taste

Peel and cut potatoes. Place in a large stock pot and cover with water. Boil until fork-tender, about 15 minutes.

Mash potatoes with butter and half-and-half.

Season with salt and pepper to taste.

Cheesy Potatoes

This is a new family favorite a made a few years ago when I had more guests than usual. It was such a hit that it is now included in the yearly feast.

---

3 lbs. Yukon Gold potatoes
1 stick butter
½ cup cream
2 cups shredded Italian 4-cheese blend
Salt and pepper

Peel and chunk potatoes into large two-inch pieces. Place in a large stock pot and cover with water. Boil until fork-tender, about 15 minutes.

Preheat oven to 350 degrees. Remove potatoes from heat, drain and return potatoes to pan. Mash potatoes with electric beater on medium low, add butter, cream, and salt and pepper to taste. Continue to mix just until ingredients are incorporated.

Place potatoes in a 9x13-inch pan. Top with cheese and bake for 40 minutes. Turn off oven to keep warm until dinner is served. This dish can be made a day ahead and baked just before dinner is ready.

Serves 6.

Scalloped Corn

This is been a favorite at Christmas dinner forever. It also goes very well as a side dish with baked ham for Easter. Actually, I love it just over a baked potato.

---

3 cans creamed corn
¾ cup heavy cream
1 cup Saltine cracker crumbs

Preheat oven to 350 degrees. Grease an 8x8-inch baking dish. In a large bowl, combine corn, cream, and cracker crumbs. Pour into baking dish. Sprinkle with salt and pepper and bake for an hour.

Serves 6 or more.

Green Bean Casserole

The classic side dish that can't be left off the holiday table.

---

5 cups cut green beans
1 cup half-and-half
1 can condensed cream of mushroom soup
1 2.8-oz. can French fried onions
Salt and pepper

Preheat oven to 350 degrees. In a medium casserole dish, mix together green beans, half-and-half, cream of mushroom soup, and ½ can of onions.

Bake for 25 minutes, or until bubbling. Sprinkle remaining onion over the top, and bake for 5 more minutes. Season with salt and pepper.

Serves 6 to 10, depending on serving size.

Sweet Potato Casserole

No canned yams here. It's so easy to bake a few beautiful fresh sweet potatoes and whip up a special addition to a delicious meal.

---

4 large sweet potatoes
½ cup heavy cream
Salt and pepper to taste
2 cups miniature marshmallows

Preheat oven to 350.

Bake sweet potatoes for 1 hour. Cool and peel. Place potatoes in large bowl and mash with cream and salt and pepper.

Place mashed sweet potato mixture in a 13 X 9-inch casserole dish and bake for 50 minutes. Top with marshmallows and bake for an additional 10 minutes.

Serves 10, depending on serving size.

Cranberry Sauce

There have been years when I've cheated and bought the canned stuff—I always regret it. This cranberry sauce is worth the extra time and can be made a couple days in advance.

---

4 cups fresh cranberries
2 cups water
2 cups sugar

Place cranberries in a medium saucepan. Add 2 cups boiling water and cover. Turn burner on medium-high and boil for 3 to 4 minutes, until the skins of the cranberries burst. Strain cranberries and put them through a ricer, reserving the juices in the pot. Return cranberries to pot with juices. Add sugar and bring to a rolling boil. Remove from heat, and cool. Store in an airtight container in the refrigerator.

Fruit Salad

We are so lucky to have fresh fruit available. My mother used to can fruit to preserve the flavors of summer. In this recipe, the whipped cream makes this dish so scrumptious even the great-grandkids gobble it up.

---

1 pineapple, cut into chunks
3 cups grapes
3 bananas, sliced
1 cup whipping cream
4 tablespoons sugar
1 teaspoon vanilla

In a large bowl, combine fruits. In a separate bowl, whip cream into peaks. Add sugar and vanilla. Fold whipped cream into fruit just before serving.

Index

www.ingramcontent.com/pod-product-compliance
Lightning Source LLC
Chambersburg PA
CBHW040855100426

42813CB00015B/2808